Shakespeare Ate My Sonnet

Peter Knaggs &
Daithidh MacEochaidh

PINP II

The Slow Moustache, Gandhi's Flip-Flop
First published in 2005 by SKREV PRESS:

    41 Manor Drive
    HEBDEN BRIDGE
    HX7 8DW

Series Editor Daithidh MacEochaidh
First Edition 2005
British Library Cataloguing in Publication Data
ISBN 1-904646-26-3
Printed by SKREV PRESS, Aberteifi
Second Edition 2007
ISBN 978-1-904646-41-9
Full details concerning SKREV PRESS, SINAP TEXTS BONES may be found at: —
www.skrevpress.com
Fourth Print Run
Cover Image
A Full English
        Nicky O'Neill

Two Collections:

The Slow Moustache
Gandhi's Flip-Flop

PETER KNAGGS hates those pretentious little bits that writers choose to write about themselves, but nevertheless feels the need to let you know that he has worked as a coleslaw shoveller in a coleslaw factory, painted Smarties, worked as a removal man, a market researcher, a mobile disc jockey, a barman and a bookseller. The most interesting reason for his dismissal has been for turning up to work in his pyjamas. He lives in Hull with his wife Annabel and two children, Holly and Daniel.

Peter has won prizes in several poetry competitions, including, The National, twice, The Bridport International, twice, and The Yorkshire Open three times. He has been published widely and very much enjoys reading his poems He is usually available for gigs.

Acknowledgements

The Author would like to thank the editors of the following publications in which some of these poems have previously appeared: The Bridport Prize Winners Anthology 2004, 'Fink,' Dress of Nettles; A Ragged Raven Poetry Competition Anthology, 'Bruce Springsteen Is Good Music To Cook Risotto To,' New Forest Poetry Competition Winners Anthology 2003, 'The 5:35 Fakenham.' Other poems appeared in: All Other Poetry is Shite, Barcode, The Consolation Prize, Gumption, Halleluah Acres, Inkpot, The North, Rain Dog, Rue Bella, The Snowman's Ears, Wet Squirrel. Scunthorpe Police Swoop on Lunatic Bean Fetish Man, was a Prize Winner in The National Poetry Competition 2004.

Two Collections

Gandhi's Flip-Flop   47

The Slow Moustache

Peter Knaggs

I would like to dedicate this book to
The Pogues and all pogues out there

The Route

Black Boy, Blacksmiths Arms, Burton Stone,
Bumper Castle, Brown Bear, Grey Mare,
Polar Bear, Bay Horse, Blue Bell, Black Bull,
Frog Hall, Golden Lion, Golden Fleece,
Golden Ball, Golden Halibut, Golden Dragon,

Golden Ferret, Three Cranes, Mucky Duck,
Red Dragon, Magpie, Buck, Tiger, Fox,
Olde Fat Goose, Corner House, Corner Pin,
Ryther Arms, Algonquin, Horse and Hare,
Horse and Hounds, Horseshoe Inn,

Hansom Cab, Roman Bath, The Flag,
The Flagon, Three Tuns, The Red Dragon,
The Griffin, The Dragon, Masons Arms,
Anglers Arms, Furious Pike, Gardeners Arms,
Photocopier Repairmans Arms,
                              The Plumbers Lock Up.

Nelson, Napoleon, The Queens Head,
The Crown, Imperial, Mitre, Henry The Eighth,
The Laughing Lion, Grobs, The Duke,
The Marquis, The George and Dragon,
Three Legged Maggot, Three Legged Mare,
                              Duelling Hares,

2

Schooner, Anchor, Five Jolly Sailors,
The Ship Inn, The Captain, Davey Jones Locker,
The Trawlermans Pension, The Octopus Reach,
The Comfy Haddock, The Albatross Tavern,
The Silver Cod, The Crab Stop, The Lobster Pot,

The Furlon, The Last Drop Inn,
The Thirsty Turtle, The Racecourse, The Horse,
The Final Hurdle, The Red Dragon,
The Red Dragon, The Yippee Club,
The Red Lion, The Local, The Glorious Pub.

Fink

Whassat, that muzzled rumble, it's a hand
in a kitchen drawer, harassing a nest of tea towels
and napkins and that solo decibel grazing
the base of my ear lobe is a cupboard hinge
opening out to scouring pads, shoe polish,
shoe brush, car wax. That tap tap tapping
like a twig against the brick, it's the riffling
through of the plastic sheaves of my compact
discs, *Shoulders, The Guillemots, Star Catcher,
Gas Bag,* unsuitable swag.

Was that gust smacking the gate shut or the
dislocated chink of a handful of our saucers being
badgered into a sack? Did you hear a clatter,
then, like crows on the tiles infiltrating
my yawny brain? It was the plasticky shake
of the electrical cord of the toaster snaked up,
handballed to a henchman with a holdall.

I'm dozy but that curt clitter scuffing the rim of
my lug could well be the final soup spoon being
shepherded into a shoplifter's pocket and I would
go back to sleep, but is that not a spot of torch
-light sailing the dresser crammed with glassware,
hunting out the prospect of silverware or
jewellery, breaching a private moment tethering
itself to the wedding photo. Listen.

4

The pickings here are uneasy pie. Through the
confines of the wash-kitchen, ferret for a scrim
to brighten the pawnbroker's eye, find light
bulbs, shed paint, garden candles. Tottle out the
cargo of my toolbox, copper wire, six inch nails,
3 amp fuses, that's all. Please go. Stop. I can hear
the groan of you sifting through the shelf
of leftover gloss, the clap of your glove
disguising your prints, and that glassy bump
is the distinct scud of *Doc Marten,*
against milk bottle, it drops and rolls
forth and back on the path all night.

Like a Shipwreck with Cannon Ball Holes

Editing the *Lugubrious Mule* has given
me ulcers, painful ulcers on my tongue,
I'm witness to their ugliness on the bent lump
of it in the bathroom mirror. It would be great
if I could unclick it, like *Lego* or a *Stickle brick*
and splosh it into a glass of cold water.
I could place it on the mantelpiece,
visitors would wince and maybe for a short while
replace it with a better tongue,
maybe that of Ted Hughes.
At readings they might appreciate my poems
more emitted in another man's voice,
then again his tongue might not have the same
conviction in the landscape of the shopping
centre, the habitat of the factory, every now
and then it might insert the word FOX
like a sestina with Tourrette's.

Maybe for comic effect I could borrow
the tongue of Bonnie Langford.
That would surprise people.
Hey, I could surprise that guy that keeps coming
in the bookshop, rubbing his stubbly jaw,
eyes on an invisible tennis match taking place
on the ceiling, *I've come for my book order,*
the names Charles, Charles Bukowski.

What about a continental tongue, Cantona

6

or Neruda, the tongue of Neruda for a night,
the words I'd share with my wife in the bedroom,
neither of us having a clue what I'm going on
about, and that would be a tongue with a talent
in another department. In the morning
I could swap back,
hoist out my pink lump, the ulcers soothed by the
dabbing on of the tincture of bicarbonate of soda,
clean, less vulgar, less foul mouthed.

Cress

It's that time of year when you rinse the swarfega
off your numb hands, chuck two *Kit-Kats*
and a pork pie into a hold all, jump the 8:20 to
Manchester Airport and chew the lid of your pen
all the way to Dewsbury thinking maybe my ink
is wasted on this country, maybe I should head to
Alicante and get away from the eggs, eke out a
line in poetry regarding *Impassioned sighs*
rocked on the cradle of the waves, instead of this
stuff about a gaje from Withernsea so sick of
eggs his thoughts are turning violent, the custard
hue of scrambled egg on toast, roast egg, boiled
egg, he's sick of the whites all runny, the yolks
overcooked, the crisp paper doily effect of those
overfried, eyelids remind him of eggshells, egg
whites the eyeball, the forsythia is the shade of
the soufflé, in dandelions and buttercups he sees
the foetus, the embryo, the ovum, the train hurtles
out of Hull-world, leaving half arsed gangsters
that pester you in pubs, offering you electric
drills, you say no, but they'll get £15 off someone
or other, which will be about a tenth of the way
towards scoring the heroin they need, that's 10
more car windows to smash or tackle with a bent
coat hanger and on the way to the dealer
pulverising the glass in every bus stop for

practise, and yesterday the front page story on
The Hull Daily Mail was about an asylum seeker
raping a British girl. Saffron, you see it in poems
don't you? But what things really are saffron?
The yolk in an egg and cress sandwich, it really
is, it can be. Eggy bread, is sometimes called
French toast or chippy toast, I love the fizzle of
the butter the dunking and the soaking of the
bread, white bread, there's a particular way of
holding the fork to whisk till the eggs blent,
there's a fine line between poaching one and
drowning it and this bloke from Withernsea, he
even sees eggs in markings by the roadside, the
egg yolk of the yellow zig zags, the egg white of
the white lines halving the road, dividing the
traffic, the way a fish slice flipping over a side of
omelette can half the pan. He's eaten so many
eggs he thinks he'll turn into a chicken if his wife
doesn't stop buying them. *Tickets please,* I pass
the conductor my ticket, he looks at it and looks
at me and passes it to me, it's stamped Hull to
Stalybridge, then I think of other things like
lemons and pancakes.

The Angler

When people ask me in libraries, how I got
started in poetry, I tell them about that time
I was fishing in the river Foss and my coffin lead
got tangled in the deadly nightshade,
so I stumbled over, my 3lb *Bayer Perlon* line
invisible, the lug worm dug from our garden
wriggling mid-air and I'm pulling my fishing line
out. I see this bottle. It's a wine bottle, all waxed
up at the top, it's muddy and inside is a note.
I take the bottle over to my rucksack
by my fishing gear and I take out my penknife
and chip at the wax. Inexpertly, I de-cork it.
The cork breaks and I end up pushing the cork
into the bottle with a porcupine quill.
I try for ages to pull up the paper. The coil
of paper has sprung out, wider than the neck.
In the end, I do get it out. On the paper is a poem.
It's about this bloke in a factory. I like it. It's
about how tired you get, how the other people
can be arseholes. I carry the bottle with me
everywhere, in my coat pocket, for the next ten
years. Then one day I'm in the *Three Legged
Maggot* and an older Scottish man engages me
in conversation. Anyhow, he notices the bottle

and asks about it. So I tell him the story, of how I
found the bottle while fishing all those years ago.
I tell him how I carry it around with me and read
the poem every now and then.
I've no idea of the author. The Scottish man
takes a look at it, reads it, and tells me
it's an early poem by the great Barnsley poet
Geoff Hattersley.
That's what I tell people, when they ask me,
in libraries, how I got started in poetry.

Doing the Dog

I thought I better tell you, arsehole, you can stick
your job, hour after hour paggering my knees,
caking my fingernails with dirt, to get pulled up
by that clever fucker for the slightest
squint of muck, my thumbnail worn to a stub
scratching up splodges of three day old
carbonara sauce or splodges of whatever stuff it
is that rich people eat and that vacuum cleaner.
Bend over son, I'll ram it right up your jacksey if
it breaks down one more fucking time. I've had it
up to here with all this, 'calm down, calm down.'
You, you smug bastard sitting pretty in your
Alpha Romeo, Thelonius Monk on your CD
player, squash racquet in the boot. Me practising
those high strokes on fag smoke, built up on the
emulsion, fugging up the gaps in the sash
windows, keeping balance, reaching out for high
spots like the pelmets and the corners of lintels,
poking out the long slim cranny of the cornice,
me pal, mopping the tide marks of the bath,
making their scum invisible, those petty notes
an' all, *Do not dust the golden Buddha today or*
  move the money tree from it's optimum west
corner Feng Shui position, gently wipe the fig
leaf tree with the blue J cloth, in the orange tub
in the right hand corner of the cupboard under

the kitchen sink. But what really gets me is those
tiny little hairs, you know the ones I mean, pubes.

Do the rich grow more than the poor? I'm sick
of picking them up, seeing them stare at me from
underneath the toilet seat, crow's nests of them,
but it were her that got to me, not him, lurking all
the time, hands on hips like a teapot.
Booked me because of our ad, *floors scrubbed in
the old fashioned manner, on hands and knees,
by maids in traditional uniform.* Well you can
swivel on this sunshine. Doggy fashion, we all
know that position and that's the position they
want me in, but I'll tell you something, I only get
in that position for one person and even for him
not that often.

Skin and Bone

Me sixteen, me, all skin , all oxblood monkey
boots, laces yellow as buttercups, all pop music
T shirts, all bone, all Walkman and tapes
lounging around on the cricket pitch, Madness
and Tracy Ullman on the radio the whole
summer. Me, all on a placement on the Youth
Training Scheme on the eighth floor of *Smartie*
packing, all cocoa up my nostrils, that smell of
firelighters in the massive lifts with those
weighty criss-cross trellised gates. Me, first day,
in the toilet cubicle cramming my pockets with
Smarties. Me, all white hygiene hat, the elastic in
the rim impressing into my skull,
me chucking it into my locker,
it feeling as though I'm still
wearing it, all tea break, pint mugs, back to it
with that that big numb old bastard, who never
wore socks or laces in his boots, who nearly got
sacked for crouching down in front of a visiting group,
and letting his bollocks fall out of the hole
in the crotch of his kecks. Me, in a department
full of girls thinking it funny too when asked, me,
sixteen, if I was a virgin, me, giving my monkey
boots a good inspection. They trained me to box
Smarties, in that glasshouse.
Smarties, they are dull when they're painted.

14

They gain that bright-as-crayon gloss when
coated with wax, that sheen, like the shine on
those lithe thighs of those twentysomething
factory girls. It was so hot they'd just strip to
knickers and bras beneath their white dust coats.
They'd cross their tantalising legs on their high
stools and didn't mind me, or forgot about me, I
was only sixteen, they had *Smarties* to box,
they'd lean forward, sideways, downwards, lift
and drop, their press studs would un-pop, I'd see
glimpses and flashes of tummy buttons, bra
straps, cleavage, sometimes that soft part at
the top of the breast, as they'd stretch or maybe
bend and those legs. I'd see frighteningly high
up. More than anything, I wanted to look, but
nothing could urge me too. Sometimes my eyes
would be facing that way, just at that moment.

Wake Me Up Before You Cocoa

I wish I could point the remote control at my
head on mornings like this and record my dreams
on video tape, then watch them, straight away.
They leap, people age instantly, metamorphosize
in a manner completely plausible to the thread of
the story. The feats in my adventures are un-
stuntman-ably impressive. The hero, usually me,
has quick wit, courage, an explosive arsenal
of martial art techniques, then there's this
strength of heart, a valiant gallant nobility
aligned to infallible wisdom, pathos, compassion.
It's as if all the worlds heroes have amalgamated
into a super Barry Sheene - Robin Hood - Geoff
Capes - Eric Bristow - Brian Jacks - Big Daddy
- Bionic - Steve Cram. Yet oddly they hardly ever
break out into a game of football, or pass a guitar
over to strum a song. Yes, I could produce my
video at that very utterance that always
precedes a monologue as dull and as predictable
as waiting for a bus in Hull on a Friday,
unstoppable once it's out, "*That they had;* delete
were appropriate, this bizarre/scary /weird/
fantastic dream *once.*" But no. My dreams desert
me, to leave me awake wishing I could go back
to that room of sleep, re-entrance halted
by butterflyed bouncers who zealously observe

the rules of admission. Annoyed that with all this
technology there's no backtracking gadget to
haul me back into my dream. That moment
of end end of journey loss, fractures
something in me, that pang. With not even
the consolation of retrieving the plot for
a blockbuster novel. The dream has gone.

Scunthorpe Police Swoop on Lunatic Bean Fetish Man

Back in Scunthorpe, police
confirmed they'd made an arrest
                         in the baked beans

case. A Scunthorpe
man has been taken into custody. Mother
is interested in this incident.
I phone her right

away. "Mother can you hear me alright?
It's been on the telly, the police
have arrested some loony.
                         Remember that incident,
that woman, barefoot, beans,
yeah, that's right mother,
they've got this fella in Scunthorpe,

in Waterstones, in Scunthorpe,
he tried it again right,
told the girl to close her eyes, mother,
poured beans on her nude foot.
                         She called the police.
The police kept some for evidence, the beans,
incidently,

this is about the seventh time, seventh incident,
all young women, in Scunthorpe,
all shop assistants, each time beans.
They think he's doing it for Comic Relief, right,
so they pull their socks and shoes off,
                                for a laugh. The police
have warned them, nowt to do with charity,
                                mother,

he's a fraud, an impostor, a nut-job, mother,
seven incidents
in the last two weeks. The police
in Scunthorpe
became suspicious when, right,
he didn't ask for any cash. He's been

known to take a photo of the bean-
smothered foot, mother.
These young lasses must be shaken. He
                                sounds like a right
weirdo. It was on the news today,
                                the latest incident.
It isn't safe to be a shop assistant in Scunthorpe.
Well it is now, now they've made an arrest.
                                The police

have bean after this beans man since that incident
in Mothercare, seven shops in Scunthorpe,
this beans nutter has hit, until now avoiding
the police.

what's the word for it? Not magic. No they are
not magic tricks, it's all real, watch, nothing in
his top hat, nothing up his sleeves, either of them.

Lines Thought to Have Been Written
Upon the Arrival of Her Bus

All dusty glass and damp cement,
Phillips screws driven into the plastic
housing of the time-tables,
the time tables soggy.

Three small counters reel out their impatient
queues while *Left Luggage,* advertises
its in house comedian.
Every major bus stop has one.

I'm drumming my fingers against my leather,
semi-whistling. The bus saunters into position,
wallops open its doors to that hiss
like opening a bottle of orangeade.

Out of the browns and greys – it's you
all yellow feather boa and green velvet
dressing gown – or so it seems

so comfortable in yourself
I expect you to be wearing slippers.
Me quickly feeling my hair is a clump
of everywhere seaweed.

It's not true to say there is a bus every ten
minutes, just that there are a simultaneous
two every twenty. It is no longer true that you
are the youngest ever person to have a number
one hit in Finland, there is someone younger.

But you look like a pop star,
even though you don't know me from Ralph,
you expect me to carry your outrageous luggage.
I couldn't think of anything more enjoyable.

Turner

For Bill Turner.

Turner thumbs the *Crown Colour Collection*
catalogue, paint for the walls, to match the sea
shell breath of the soft lime curtains,
there's something bucolic about the soapy apple
mint, it's like Monday. Da de da, there's
something ferocious like washing up liquid
of the forest pine non drip gloss, but
would it go with his croc skin boots,
his nettle weave strides, his broccoli soup?
He could darken it up to canal boat or cucumber
skin, or something between moss and seaweed,
with the hue more towards crayon than duck
shite, but not too bellicose or military,
then something mellow for the skirting,
soft boiled cabbage, tinted by a quartzy
avalanche or muzzy grasshopper, would it match
the ferocious ivy of the settee?
Dum de dum, a tin of topiary, rain washed
herb garden, swarfega suffused
into thrustling dock leaf, emulsion, bolder
brighter Turner, verdant turf, grass, gloss,
the avacado of his third newest shirt.
Turner think of the daylight changing to
lamplight, the pen on the peppermint of the page
the dappled caterpillar felt of the moon,

filtered through the wine bottle green
of the window, it's thirsty work all this,
just choose something to remind you
of the hills or conker trees, pour
yourself a drink in your emerald glass Turner,
maybe a drink of orange or something.

A Donkey and an Oak Tree in a Field in a Photo
For Peter Lewin

Primus the donkey in a field,
Primus the donkey one hundred years old,
compass-needle nose homing on the shaggy
umbrella of the oak.

Primus hauls in and expels
the great cold Yorkshire air, in his life-fence,
his field, bare as a freshly-sheared-lamb, baa,
Primus, to munch

the harvest down
till spring. Then to start again. Saddled
with the pure nonchalance of an old barn.
To meet the rain

like a cousin, there,
hay barn hewn into the crest of the hill.
It pours a robe of rain, smoothes the fur
like a lotion

the sun to dry
it like hay. Primus mortised in the saddleback
of the hill, hoof forward, the bulk of his grass
full stomach

the stove of his life,
fuel for the tightrope of his muscles, taut
between the cartwheel shoulders and the rifle-
butt-hind.

Hooves
washed in mud. Muggard. He's hung there
poised for a page in a picture book or postcard.
Primus is a donkey,

hee haw, badged
for a tot and child cargo, toy employment.
Pensioned, put out to pasture, so flies
can perform

acrobatics, muster
on the tee-pees of his ears, flit the swamp
of nostril flesh, tripping the pin-cushions
of his frequent whiskers.

Pelt of fur, clop of hoof ,
bark, branch, leaf. Stable mate veterans pinned-
up and penned into mill-life, good companions.
Primus and the oak

tree, ready
for the hiker to pass them by, tomorrow
filling his footprint with his foot
on a different path.

Primus will twitch
his ropey tail, starfish-eyelashes locating
on the retina some swirl in the oak,
in the bark,

or on the hill beyond, or on the hill beyond.

Display This

It is a poster for a poetry reading by Alan P.
Penguin. One night only, as part of the, Church
of the Pentecostal & Christian Aid Goat Appeal.
The plan is to purchase goats for widows in
Burundi, Central Africa. The poetry reading is
the star attraction of their six week fundraising
programme. It is un-missable because Alan P.
Penguin is supported by a, "*Multi-instrumentalist
with a voice like an earthy angel,*" Astrid
Anderson. "*Her solo debut album, Scunthorpe 6
New York 0, recorded over a six months, 3
months in a basement in New York,
3 months in a basement in Scunthorpe, is a
startlingly original mix of vibrant simplicity and
charged intensity.*" themes echoed in the poetry
of Alan P. Penguin.

He will be reading from his three self-published
books, "The Bird In The Dappled Light,"
"Iridescent," and "The Selected Poems
of Alan P. Penguin. Alan's poetry has been well
received and attracted a number of reviews. Alan
says, "My poetry deals with a range of emotions
and subjects in a variety of styles. Doncaster is
present and periphery... Writing isn't my job."

A specially commissioned, limited edition selection, "Goat Poetry," has been produced for the appeal and will be available on the evening. Tickets are Â£4, which includes wine, doors open 7:30pm.

NB: Alan P. Penguin will be available from 7:00pm for a photo opportunity.

Thrash Metal is the New Trout

It does something for me, to see a grrrrl with bare
arms play a guitar, fast, like a sprat thrashing on
the deck of a trawler, to plunge into the sound-
scape and wheel back. *The Old Bell* dartboard
chalked down to 51 and double 17. Her 30 odd
bracelets jig as she trampolines the platoon
of her strings, clobbers and bosses the music into
an angry live box. It bazookas out and into our
heads through the bass bins, the speakers the plug
holes of our ears. *Codswallop,* the Newfoundland
band who have a manifesto of publicising
Canada's theft of the world's cod.
They're getting to the big hit single,
"I don't want to be fishless."
the mosh-pit is writhing with dudes clouting each
other with haddock and chubb. At the back
they're releasing stowaway bream and ling
from their unbuttoned shirts. Wow. She marmalizes
that guitar, pounding it. I'm removing the sea
bass from my trousers. It's nearly time. It's
all badly taped together with that roadies' silver gaffa
tape, then the strobe lights flicker on and we're
all stars of our own black and white movie.

Bruce Springsteen is Good Music
to Cook Risotto to

but the phone rings. It's Banana Dave.
Do I fancy a pint in five minutes?
Course I do. By the time I'm necking
the first of the night, the risotto is yet

to stop bubbling. Banana looks old.
His nose drops down like a courgette stub.
His nostrils are like fireplaces. Arsenal,
he thinks, will win the league. The charts are crap,

full of manufactured shite. His skin falls
into his gob like a shirt falling off
an ironing board. His cheeks are pushed in
like thumbed in milk bottle tops. Banana tells me

every thing's alright, every thing's ok, you know.
It takes him five pints to get round to it.
It's the house. He can't go back to the house,
it just feels so empty, now his mam's gone.

Martin Sitting In The Dining Room

His ears are a pair of plastic saucers
each melted on a different side, they
seem to big for his whole face, which
seems burnt by life, the scorch of it
singeing the youth from his combed
back hair, whiting at the seams, a
distorted letterbox of a mouth open.
Labelling his nose, a knob of molten
metal puddled from the furnace, welded
there. His features twist like a coat
pulled from the river and dumped
on the bank, the colour of a King
Edward potato, his forehead disp-
laying a cochineal map of a third
world country, all of it, to the sinewy
tree stump of his neck somehow
inserted into a laundered shirt with
a stiff collar. Martin is sitting sideways
on a metal chair, too unreal, but the
anguished cave roof of his eyebrows
betray his emotions. His eyes implore
me to understand the crux of things.
Martin is sitting in the dining room.
He can't talk, but he is communicating.

The Egg and Spoon Races

Now we've got this far bouncing tennis balls
in the air, sixteen, seventeen, on a cricket bat,
the flat side, eighteen, heading that way,
nineteen, with our left legs tied to each other,
deely boppers on our heads, Neds Atomic
Dustbins yellow splodge logo splatting our
t-shirts, careful Ziggy don't drop
the tennis ball, we've got this far, the length
of a reel of tape, one of those that scares you a bit
with its whiplash as it recoils into its housing
and you might use it to measure the twelve inch
length of the leaf engraved front door window,
broken, on both sides, don't twenty four wet
the putty with water. Use linseed oil
and once the putty is thumbed in take a knife
and scratch it flat, otherwise, for years you'll
twenty seven be left staring at a load of thumb
prints in a line, a sign that along the line
something changed in this house.

The 5:35 Fakenham

Eddie Freemantle and Graham Rock both tip
Red Hare, but I can't help thinking it's time
Tony McCoy rode another one home.
We've gone through the card nearly.
I'm well up on the day, my horses keep winning
so I stick a few quid on number seven,
Leader Supreme. Under starters orders,
and they're off. *Red Hare* leads from the start,
Tony McCoy's in the middle of the pack
but there's a long way to go,
two miles and four furlongs to be exact
and not many horses lead the field from starting
blocks to winning post and Tony McCoy
gains ground but *Red Hare* is ahead
by two lengths and a half. As they pass
the crowds on their first circuit
Tony McCoy on *Leader Supreme* puts on a bit of
a show with a bit of a spurt and they're neck and
neck, head to head and *Leader Supreme* is taking
the lead, white stars embossed onto emerald
green and that excitement rushes through me,
the excitement that my horse might come in,
as hoof kicks up turf and they're curving
the turn of the final lap, coming up the inside
railings is the outsider *Nibbles,* he's closing fast
but *Leader Supreme* is still a length in front
at the final furlong, one fence to jump
and *Nibbles* is putting up a strong challenge

37

and *Red Hare* is still among the frontrunners,
they take the final fence together and *Leader
Supreme* has fallen, it's *Red Hare* who swerves
round the fallen McCoy and propels himself to
the finishing line to take first prize and
I can't believe it. Good job I chose to put
a few quid on it as well.
It's always the best feeling to take some dough
off the bookies especially in the last race of the
day, and I'm waiting with my baby daughter by
the ladies and supping off the end of my pint
smiling like the jockey and owner in the winners
enclosure, waiting for my wife. I smile at my
baby. From her pushchair Holly smiles her head
off at me and suddenly everything seems so easy.

The Glass Octopus and the Muesli Jellyfish

The jellyfish blobber and wibble
their swimmy way across the ocean
of the wall, I could sit here all day
in this museum and watch the projection,
it's like an executive relaxation class,
but the *Nova* is on a meter and still
an exhibition of glass sea life to wander round.
My girl wants to stay with the jellyfish,
but we drag her round the crafted glass
of sea-cucumber, sea-snails, squids.
I imagine myself pulling melted glass
with a pair of pliers, manipulating
tentacles, fish tails, swans' necks.
A voice pounces out of the museum quiet,
"This is boring. I want to go to the pub."
It's my girl, she's two.
This morning she was watching the *Tweenies,*
when I shuffled in. 'Daddy look at this.'
On the coffee table, the perfect bowl of the head,
the wobbly dragged fingers of the legs,
'Look at what I've made. It's a muesli jellyfish'.

Just Shopping

It was only when my mobile phone
tootled in my carrier bag, I looked
down and the bag was moving,
I started to suspect, had my hand pecked.
Now we're circling the kitchen table
all staring at this chicken, strutting,
blinking, clucking, scratting, pondering
methods of execution, helpful Jellicoe's
up for twisting its neck as a *Rubik's* cube,
then I've got the head on the breadboard
and the carving knife to its neck,
I shouldn't dither and dally, do it,
right quick. I just asked for a chicken,
a normal chicken, wondered why
the butcher were taking so long
out back, he came back with this bag,
now I'm here, my wife screaming,
not on the bloody breadboard,
me seriously considering my future
custom with that quality butcher's.

A Lunch Time Errand Disrupted
by Bank Robbing Guinea Pigs

I've got some savings to deposit
into my account. Lunch hour finds me
in the queue at the building society,
notes tucked into my paying in book.

The door is barged open by three
guinea pigs. I'd like to be more descriptive
but they were wearing balaclavas.
They don't join the queue, they push in,

scuttling under the queue barrier,
one of them is armed with a sawn-off
shot gun, one is armed with a revolver.
They have a note demanding a sum

of money, there's an explosion, a crash
barrier drops to protect the building society
employees, except one has her hand severed,
it drops onto the floor this side of the counter.

The guinea pigs are supremely racked off,
they start popcorning, firing their guns,
this causes most of the customers to dive
onto the floor. I run up and boot a robber,

his comrades try to shoot me, they squeek
something that sounds like, " eekaletar eek
eek ank eek adish leaves eek eek spunt."
Next thing they're heading for the glass door.

41

One of them shoots me in the lower arm.
Well, I think, my customers won't be happy
about this, this afternoon, me dripping
blood all over their merchandise.

Stone of a Peach

It's been a while since his fingers
have twisted a spigot. When he thinks
about it it's like a bubble in his windpipe
trapped like a marble in a straw
that he can't cough up, or cough out
and the sherry nurses his injuries
and the cider dresses his wounds,
they're bandaged and dressed and bandaged
and dressed to the extent they can't heal
unless they're all untied to expose
a fresh wound. He is scruffy and dirty
and his face is the stone of a peach.
It is correct. Treading breath first
his feet are reluctant to follow
the squalor of his trousers, the debris
of his kicked and clouted coat,
the slouch poking a route to a smudgy horizon
via the margins of *Miss Selfridges, Starbucks,
HMV, Waterstones, French Connection,*
the public steering clear of his road,
him coveting the perfume of washed skin
and a bed in a nice hotel just for one night.
Only waging an anti-deodorant war
because if he scrounged enough change
the one thing he wouldn't spend it on
right now is a tin of *Lynx* or any deodorant.

Government Policy

Take two boys the same age,
give one a crap job, one no job,
no house, the ground to sleep on
under an arch, give one a cohort,
a surfeit of aftershave, a Friday,
give the other a pocket full of coins,
no bank account, the last two copies
of *The Big Issue,* give one compassion,
the wrong one, put one in the path
of the other this Friday, perambulating
or sleeping, give one enough
but make him hungry, give one a shave,
the other a weather-scoured face
like dirty upholstery, malnourished.
Nourish the other one on violence,
give him a street full of bars, nobody
to talk to, counterfeit friends with
seven pint brains, girls advertising sex
but not selling any, spoil ones control
panel, watch him and his mates
drive the other into his lightless asylum,
give him no one to bail him out
so he can only surrender to the sting
of their kicks and afford to curl out
of his ball when they're at the kebab hut,
one handing over the otherone's money.

The Quick Moustache

The road is rocky, but the road isn't very long.
The road is rocky but not as rocky as the lane.
The road is rocky, he fell out with the bypass.
The road is lonely but not as lonely as the quarry.

The road is rocky, but the road isn't very long.
The road is rocky but the verge is nice and soft.
The road is rocky but the grass is a nice
soft cushion. The road is long and great fun for geologists
of all ages.

The road is lonely, perhaps he needs a good companion
(like a friendly hound or a sociable horse)
The road is rocky, but the road isn't very long.
The roadworks have been traffic coned off
and the tailbacks are gonna be long,
tailbacks are gonna be long, are gonna be long.

The road is rocky, but I'm not on an
uncomfortable pony and trap.
The road is rocky but the grass is nice and blue.
The road is lonely but not as lonely as the
graveyard. The road is rocky but it won't be rocky for long.
The road is rocky but the steamroller won't
be long.

In That Direction

Go past Pound Land, past Everything
For a Pound, by Pound Squeezer,
Pound Finder, Pound Pincher,
Pound Pounder, Pound Squasher,
Pound Basher, Pound Pound Pound,
make a beeline for It's a Quid,
turn right at Purveyors of the Finest
Quality Gifts For a Pound, it's
next door to Mighty Pound. If you
reach Pound Fayre turn round, too far,
go back to The Quid Squad opposite
Wonder Pound, turn right at Planet Pound,
go on by Poundemonium, One Pound
Please, One Pound Please Sir, One
Pound Please Madam, The Original
Pound Shop, by that one that was there
first, The Pound Zone, up past A Pound
It Is and there you go, there you have it,
there it is, Everything You Need 10p.

Gandhi's Flip-Flop

Daithidh MacEochaidh

Also by Daithidh MacEochaidh

Like a Dog to its Vomit

Half a Pint of Tristram Shandy

Travels with Chinaski

Solipsism for Beginners

Ramraid

Islands in Time

Life & Death of an E-Book

Liquorish Durg

48

DAITHIDH MACEOCHAIDH poet, short-story-writer, novelist and publisher, born in Scunthorpe, educated at Hull, York (Ripon and St. Johns) and Huddersfield. He has lived in every riding of Yorkshire, but not for a bet. There seems to be an invisible twine that keeps drawing him back to the land of Tykes, for he has also lived in Ireland, Scotland, Wales — which sounds like the beginning of a retro-seventies joke, but isn't. He now lives on the side of a hill with his much better half, two bairns, currently, one seven years, the other twelve weeks, and various broken printers. He may soon have to give up writing and publishing to look for a proper job.

DEDICATED to ma cousin Chris —
who couldn't give a toss

"Everything in this world, said my father, is big with jest,"
Sterne, L., 1961, *Tristram Shandy*, London, Everyman

1 Dutiless@Zinderneuf

… we found ourselves waking
to find morning already woken
getting along quite fine without us …

"Some poets write asking for quotes for their books
Daithidh MacEochaidh writes with suggestions:
   'Stop bothering me!'
   'This bloke needs locking up!'
Well he probably does
or we all do.

His poetry will astonish you:
uninhibited energy to the power^3
He's unstoppable."

    David Morley
    Director: Warwick Writing Programme
    University of Warwick

51

NEW ORDER

Covert operations secured Dumbo's ears,
hijacking in technicolored stereophonic
to glide over the towers of Disney's Castle,
taking it all, swifter than the CIA,
faster than marines, speedier than Gonzalez,
Captain America or supersonic Superman.
We took it all.
      First job, we failed to make a man
of Mickey Mouse, couldn't take his pitch
no more. Second job, we took it in turns
to put the burkah on Cinderella
now you see her, another fella
Third job, Peter Pan walking the swingometer
by satellite — the modern way to fight
a war. War took it all.
      We had other jobs to do when we lost,
lost it all, lost the war. We asked for
Geneva, our mothers, the rule of law,
even as they made us worship an infinite
line of Marilyn Monroes, fed every fifteen
minutes on Campbells soup, washed down
with Coke. Sometimes a MacDonald,
fries on the side. Worse, making us witness
the new junta driven to power. They'd
trussed up Daffy Duck, goose-stepping
proud as a Pinochet, just as quackers.
Won. They'd won, as we hummed along
to a Fred Quimby Cat and Mouse
National Anthem, knowing that we had
found at last the home of the free   joke.

KADISH

Thick as pig-shit
never knew Matty Levitz
was a Yid.
Owed Porker Sullivan
dinner money for cigs
Found him by the shops.
Took him to the swings.

Levitz couldn't pay his dues
till I held his hand in mine
behind his back as Sullivan
cracked his nose, smacked his lips.
Left him with pockets rifled
no hue of lie in his wail,
"An't got no money!"

Never knew he was kosher
till we walked away, moneyless,
but all debts paid, as Levitz,
voice breaking, sang the Kadish,
that twisted ma heart behind
ma head, Sullivan felt bad too,
"But after all," he said, "He jewed us!"

SOMETIME

Shaun tied time on his hands,
measuring the queue at the Job Centre
holding a carriage clock, works gone,
calls it symbolic—no name for a clock.
Shaun's nay bothered, cut to a nano-second
routine: makes inadequate sex to next door
neighbour, arrives home in time to take
the top off his boiled egg. All worked out
though the second hand went AWOL at New Year
when they called time anually, as he forgot
to make a revolution. But as nowt as to when
the hour hand dropped off as they took
his dog away to take up smoking, full time
at the local laboratory—at least someone
in the household was working, everything timed out
written down and noted, even to the precise hour,
minute and second, cutting up the earth,
the dog's lungs, a huge lopsided blood grapefruit
nay special spoon for the job, headless boiled egg,
not that any of this counted, when the Claims
Adviser asked how come he turned up early.
Shaun has time on his hands, a signature on his bru
blobbing on paper, the blood of a dog but
he still misses those handy hours, minutes
and seconds left uncounted, queing quietly,
politely behind tomorrow.

CHANGING CHANNELS [1]

Father marked him first, for when he sneaked in
he did not put the door home and the fire began to smut.
Father shook his paper, complained of the draft, "Put
wood in't t'ole, lad!" said Father. He did that.

He just stood against the wall, ragged hole in his neck,
mother wondering whether he'd wiped his feet on't step.
He never woh what you would call tidy. "Flipping heck,
I'm dead, tha knows - dead!" he said. But that's no help.

Eventually, Jean and her new-to-her boyfriend, Donal,
budged up a bit on't settee and he took a seat.
He tried to mek conversation, asked what been happening this week.
No one took him on. There woh this film playing and it woh diabolical.

It weren't worth watching, but we watched all t' same.
Father ruffled his paper, Jean and Donal
necked a bit and mother thought about changing the channel.
But he seemed suddenly engrossed, her murdered son,

"It's not like that!" he said, raised his voice and all.
"All that tv violence, dying, gasping out last words,
gentle closing of eyelids — all wrong, absurd!"
He would have gone on, but mother bad him hush.

Father gave him a Paddington stare from over the top
of his newspaper — banked on a snooze after his Sunday Dinner.
And I knew he wanted to say more, to tell his father
for once in his life that he woh talking rot and had allus talked rot.

Father said not a word, just glared; the credits rolled.
Father asleep, Mam put kettle on and Jean said
it woh time that she walked Donal home. "How's it going, arr Kid?"
I asked just to be social, but we'd never got on ever since I sold

his *scarelectrix* down t' market. He'd done wi' visiting.
Father woke when he slammed home the front door.
"Just in time," said Mother, "Shall I pour?"
Mother handed around the cups and a couple
of slices of best Yorkshire Parkin.

Into the corner

had Van Gogh's ear on a key
ring, it didn't glow in the dark,

didn't paint much, had these
mad wiry grey, ginger-grey,
hairs, bristling out the hole,
dipped ma pen into
that curl of darkest, then write
the craziest shopping lists:

1 Hitler's testicle
1 Pol Wittgenstein's hand
2 Django Reinhardt fingers
2 Duggy Bader's legs
3 Rolf Harris' wigs

Never could afford
the messages
no matter that I
couldn't spell
or even, a door home
for ma key

making a pig's ear
of Poet Scratchings
last a week

HAND OF MARADONNA [2]

Had death on ma hand
puckered up with new scar tissue
came to a priest to talk it through,
disturbed him trying to glue
a hand on a fallen virgin Mary,
said that *Superglue*
would do the trick, but really
a bit fiddly, held the hand
of God's mother in place
while your man went at haste
with bitten fingernails and paste
So grateful that I could help out,
even got a cup of tea and biscuit waste,
a holy trinity teapot with a pope spout.
When it dried, when I moved my hand
couldn't see the join between parts
wholesome as the sacred heart
— a bloody miracle — *Superglue.*

HOME SHOPPING [3]

Lidls just watching cheap alphabetic
spaghetti, assailed by piped music from the Second
Viennese School, some elegant waltzing
reductive propositions, self-evident as the
reductions in Lidl's own *Premium High Juice*
discounted, and minding my own commercial activity
to comment to the girl of the till that they no longer
stocked them peppers from Hungary, perhaps
it was the sub-text or bad grammar
because she invited me outside
to go goose-stepping toe-toe with the theme song
of 2001 Space Odyssey; she won by two flights
of the Valkeries and a kick in ma latent supplementary
jouissance to my rather condensed version of
Nietzsche's eternal recurrence and sultanas. She agreed
to let go, provided I paid cash for three sublimed
special offers, which took the change from a
credit card, leaving me something with which
to greet next week, when peppers
might stage a come back and the spaghetti spell
out ma destiny, at some affordable recompence.

CHINASKI'S SHANTY — IN THE EARL DE GREY [4]

for Dave the Kipper — a gud drink owed

Henry Chinaski and Dave the Kipper
from Boston were having this drinking
competition. The Kipper winning.
Chinaski hated it, hated him, hated
the way drink drank him in, then spat him out.

There's no beating the Kipper:
hand-pulled pint is sea-foam,
tart whiskey, salt tang of sea-spray,
stranded souls of seagulls keen
through the skulls of passing bar-keeps:
Time on your glasses now please!
Chinaski tried to dib the Kipper a sly one.
Dave took Chinaski's knuckles, held onto
the five sweating digits, and tried to gain
again the measure of his sea-legs,
as he bucked feeling swell, dropping
to the dregs of doldrums, marooned by land.

Something thirsty and wanting
in the sea-spilling neap-tide of his glass
stranded till the next, wet with lostness;
Chinaski's hate held tightly in hand
anchoring the sap of storm rise some lost
albatross seeking numb comfort of the one-
eyed whore pulling tricks in the corridor
to the gentlemen's and fruit machine.
And Henry Chinaski knows he'll win.
Dave the Kipper still stands the next round,
three years overboard late last spring.

2 SUGARS BUT NO MILK [5]

She rapped, she raged, she belted
on ma door; wouldn't mind
but it was open. She stood five foot
five in bedroom slippers, naked but
for her hair in Andy Cap curlers — a most
inauspicious sign. She said have you
been using ma toothbrush? I shook
ma head. Considering she was an
imperfect stranger, I thought that
there was a good chance that
I was in the clear. She said don't
invite me in then. I didn't.

At a quarter past five, she was back,
with her husband, slippers, shitty
jocks and a purple string vest. Go on,
Harry, sort the twat she said. The man
warned me that he was Salvation Army trained.
I nutted him in the false teeth. She said
are you going to invite me in or not.
Booting her fallen husband out of the way
I managed to close the door on this for at least
two days. She was back, dressed this time
with something from the HOPE charity shop.
She said that she was sorry and all that,
her husband was sorry and all that,
and it wouldn't happen again but that
I shouldn't mess with her toothbrush
and that's a fact, leaving me gob-smacked
with minty breath.

K-BABBED

For Leo the Greek

walked in the job
like a wounded trochee
giving it the big I-am-bic
something penned into
a forethought in 9/sick slip
jigging off time and half after
12.00 a.m and all the grease
you can eat, Ancient or Modern,
serving up chips off the shoulder,
a chilli-thriller source of food
poisoning, never promising
Turkish Delight, it Kurdled
in his stomach, with nay questions
aspirated, nay breathless tarrahs
to the short-skirted legs walking out,
shouting potential hangovers into
the street, about the cheek of wogs
raping them with their butcher's eyes,
wiping sweat on the apron, by the
back of his underhand employment
status, wondering over the hiatus
atween pub and night club throwing
up, taxi battles, boozed up violence
pished into the night, still managing
to call in for something spilled
down the black shirt front,
nay questions axed with a shut
mouth catching the flies around
the neon trap, flying tonight
into tomorrow, some tomatoes,
bit of green, bit of a wage
coming in and never a syllable
of thanks, not a smidge, and by
heckles he knows he's hateful

walking out into a nice clean
van that smells of dogs down
to a depot where a woman
has waited up all these hours
to pronounce his name right
off the label on his ticket flight
back

2 Mills & Bust

...Knut Handsome,
String Theory Guru
From the 11th
dimension
has at last
slipped the knot ...

...the texture of the everyday world
with inventive craft and a sense
of humanity

Black Mountain Review

63

HULL REVISITED — RELUCTANTLY [6]

Couldn't 'credit' it taking the 420 to Ashington
for the price of £1.75 return to find masel' in Hull,
a universe away where Philip Larkin is a
card carrying Stalinist in love with the working
classes and as far as booze is concerned
an abstainer of the purest water, pushing
his aged parents in a pram around Newland Park,
lovingly tucking in their blankets, saying hello
to everyone, thinking about his next poem
for the New Statesman. Seemed strange to find
masel' again in Hull even if it now looked like
Harrogate, prosperous, geared up large
as a snug, smug, southern retirement home.

As for masel', enough of the poetry circuit,
I'm one of Prime Minister Scargill's men,
on a gravy train south shutting down
all the obsolete merchant bankers, stock markets
and financial institutions, nay redundancy
nay golden handshake, just a one way ticket
to certain out of the way Siberian salt mine.

I could be here a long while, could be wrong,
'cos in this world the busses and trains
run on time, a bit like Mussolini and Italy
without the good weather or the smell of cod.

EIRIGI SUAS BRIGANTAIGHE [7]

So I wasn't in the 'York Arms'
when this never happened:
This Gaje, says yon man up at the bar, was walking down
Micklegate like this: here his fingers —
Mimic a pair of mincing legs, skipping at the
fingertips — tha knos what I mean.
When, says yon man, this gang of nobb-heads start teking
the piss — just layking mindst —
but, says yon man, this Gaje teks umbrage,
runs amok, goes berserk: from bern serkr,
bear's skin, Old Norse.

So I popped in after blobbing-on the bru, having a
wee one in the 'York Arms', hearing
this story of a rather camp hard man kicking the crap
out of a gang of the head-the-balls on the Micklegate
run: pint in every pub and puking just for puffs.

And I start to think about all that Old Norse carving
up the city:
Walmgate
Micklegate
Gillygate
Monkgate
Whip-ma-whop-ma Gate:
short on steps
long on words.

All that Viking cant ingrained like muck when ah woh
nobbut a bairn layking, fighting, falling out
and meking mates without a care for words, dialect, history —
Gata, meaning street and Eric Bloodaxe never a man
to mince his words; Caer Ibrac, Brythonic York;
the vanished Celt, Roman, Norse and the Angle
whom endured I raised my jar of Yorkshire Ale to —
those whom had come, seen, saw, and gone afore:
Sláinte! ah says, then the tongue of the Ancient Brits,
Iechyd da!

65

When the barman turns, concerned, asks,
Hvordan står det til?
Suddenly, empty glass, love of words, walk out, history shouting
over my shoulder:
Takk bra!

THE KIPPER'S SHANTY [8]

Dave the Kipper from Boston
was a hard cunt and there's no
denying that, example, one time,
he taking on this Kale Budhru,
this Trinidad stick fighter and winning —
the Kipper didn't even have a stick.

By fuck he could drink
one of those gajes that drinks
and drinks and never gets pissed
though he tried hard when his
ship docked, flocking to the brothels
not that he always shagged, sometimes
he just went along for the crack,
said to me all brothels were the same
just like the sea allus changes
and nobody knows the weight of water
this earth carrying, the way it weaves
and works upon the mind.

He liked brothels though, that was the place
to take a look at your fellow man, woman
and those who couldn't make up their minds;
seen it all: black whores, yellow whores,
white whores in Hamburg who'd shame
any Hollywood star or catwalk princess;
said he got high smelling the stink
of sweat, spunk and cunt — the only way
he could get off in those days when he
couldn't get drunk, merely quiet.

But that all changed one time
outside Capetown laid up and suffering,
fever, shakes possibly dying, waking
to find this spanner-basher mate
giving him good head.

After that something was gone,
something lost in his sea-shuffle,

he wasn't a gay basher, nothing like that,
once had a Filipino tranny lover, six
weeks laid up waiting for his ship to come in,
but something had gone and strangely
he could get drunk, ever day gobbling
a bottle of whiskey down, every day
spitting, shitting or pissing a bit more
of his mind away till he got sacked
some place States-side on the East Coast
and the embassy had to fly him back
from this hospital after they found
him knifed by a taxi-rank.

He's back now for good, sometime soon
I promise myself to see that man
take a trip to Boston *Lincs*, fry him
some kippers for breakfast
pour him a good drink
wait till his words beach up
on the strand of my own mind,
out there beyond the breakers
sinking beneath the weight the oceans.

SINCEREST FORM – LES DAWSON IS IAN MCMILLAN [9]

Ah didn't pop mi clogs yon neeght last ...
whenever, ah woh only joshing.
Ah just wrapped mi old Working Men Club
suits and shirts around mi swineway piano.
Thumbed a lift from a milk float
that woh health-food running the border
atween Lancashire and Yorkshire.
Driver says, 'Hey, tha's—'
'Appen tha reet lad, ah'm Ben Elton.
Ah'm not really working class,
ah've bin faking it, despite elocution lessons
in Cockney from Dick Van Dyke.
'Ollreet lad! Don't go on!' says the driver,
as we pulled up on the front by the pier at Barnsley.

The rest is history:
colliers coming home from redundancy
soberly singing, "Men of Horlicks";
judging a poetry competition
handing out prizes;
grin, smile, shek hands
and say, 'Here's thi Blankety-Blank
Cheque-Book and Pen!' - laugh from
audience, think it's irony.

Ah sit here supping Yorkshire beer,
getting bigger and better:
ah'm Ted Booze,
ah'm Les Dawson,
ah'm Ian Macmillan.

Aye, ah guess
tha's reet
any fact will do.

BREAKING THE ICE AT A MONDAY CLUB SOIREE [10]

Step 1

hold one pink gin in one's hand
turn,
turn face the High Church Anglican 'Priest' and
quiz,
quiz him on the cup size of the average angel's
bra

Step 2

reach over and take a handful
of assaulted peanuts and assorted tit-bits
seek out the loud lady in a purple
rinse and annual holder of the Hunt Ball,
ask her if she is so posh that she
gets out of the bath
to pee

Step 3

fall down
fall up
piss in the punch
puke on the couch
pick a fight with the homophobic
Captain of the rugga-team
accuse of being
a born again bugger
and a cut-price closet-queen

Step 4

toast the Queen

Step 5

put out Queen
using prescribed fire-fighting appliance

Step 6

70

blow nose on old school tie

Step 7

return old school tie from whom thou hast borrowed
the aforementioned item and scratch bottom
showing obvious relief, perhaps exclaim
"Oo! My Farmer Giles!"

Step 8

discuss new age travellers
poachers and trespassers against us
with Farmer Giles —
if particularly vexed
suggest the use of twelve bore

Step 9

suggest
put away twelve bore
or
reload bloody sharp
and shoot the fuckers

Step 10

agree:
bring back
Capital Punishment
and 'Upstairs, Downstairs'
on a Sunday evening,
there's never punishment enough
even including 'Songs of Praise'

Step 11

take out
cheque-book
wait to have
back slapped

Step 12

make out a cheque
for a real biggy
wait to have
back slapped again
and decline several offers of marriage
from some of Britain oldest families
of Bankruptocracy

Step 13

make cheque
payable to
Tony Blair

Step 14

sign with love and hugs
from
Arthur Scargill

Step 15

leave to cheers
put on bicycle clips
steal BMW
drive home with clogs on
wait for knighthood
put on the co-co.

THAT FLIP-FLOP THANG

for the lad, himsel'

when Knaggsey used a pet phrase of mine,
took it for a walk around a sextet
like a mustachio twirling Victorian villanella,
I wasn't as arsed as Bernard Manning, but when
it got praised off the cuff, I rolled back
ma Vic Reeves, miffed, despite it being
a good poem, leaving me feeling as
down at heel as Jesus's underpants —
not quite as slick as Gandhi's flip-flop
not quite as clear as to what it says, but
at least safely mine, kennelled in the backyard,
under-praised with all ma other pet phrases
pining for a poet to give them decent work

TO OBSESS [11]

Obsession is not a perfume by Calvin Klein
it's knowing you still prefer sex with the maniac
who kicked your teeth out.

Obsession is reiving your dirty knickers
from the washing basket, sniffing
for another man's cum.

Obsession is sharp, brittle tears
broken into the night, stale with loneliness
indulgent as masterbation.

Obsession is burning every letter, photograph
and scrap of happiness, opening windows to waft
acrid hatred and lingering despair.

Obsession is to wither to the bone
to shrink to the tentative first ape-step to earth
to beat, shriek and howl with fear unknown.

Obsession is grinding my nose into your hair
wanting to kick you downstairs, break your ribs and teeth
to savour the smell of that good sex you had elsewhere.

Obsession is nay perfume, but the verb infinite
                                        that
and the cold stink of the heart.

74

THE MISSIONARY POSITION

We lost it all at the Council
of Whitby, up on the hill
by the car park, screams of gulls.
Apparently, we got our tonsures
inside out, the Irish front pate was
not the fashion in Rome, worse
was when they separated monks
from nuns, apparently St Augustin
had long been against that sort
of thing, instead they re-described
our bodies for us along with a new
cut and trim at the back: penis,
vagina, semen, scrotum — we now
had Latin bodies that we didn't ken
what to do with or even if we did
weren't allowed to return to our
strange bastard Angle-Celt kirkways.
'Load of balls,' said sister Urmstwald,
'Let's have cock, cunt and cum!'
— the thump of alliteration —
as we turned peasant, graved the common
furrow with our own words,
reaping dialect stubborn with skulls.

JUNK-MAIL [12]

We made love without the need
for double glazing.
We bonked without the need
of several banks' platinum credit cards.

We managed good sex
without the need
of a new car every year
or a dishwasher, latest model.

When our child came along
we sent him/her out into the world
with a cardboard box, begging bowl
and some nondescript hound
on a piece of second-hand string.

We still made love
without all the modern necessities,
but knew it was time for a change
when our eldest became
a double glazing salesperson.

NO ANGLO-SAXONS, NO WHITE PROFESSIONALS, NO PET-HATERS

There's room in ma heart
but could be bigger.
I'm renting by the throb,
beat and bounce of blood.

I've had offers in the past,
regret them all. I've even
had to turf out squatters,
or cheating fuckers who'd
no longer pay their dues
or cunts that had wrecked
the place, ripped out ma prick,
pissed on ma sexual confidence,
sprayed on the wall how shit
I was in bed, afore they ran off,
taking the telly and the stereo
leaving me to pay off the higher
purchase and the rest of the debt.

But that nothing, but that nowt,
compared to this thief, this
choring tchai, betti monisha,
who came one night and
took the whole damn room, she took
it all, aye, all, leaving me
just the space and nay
punters interested in a
man with nothing
in his heart.

3 Machines of Joy Inc. - Batteries not Included

...Mrs Louis Althusser's Last Word: —

You stuck my neck
out
for your principles
and
it hurt.

And on that theme, there's something madly likeable about MacEochaidh's writing, a kind of exuberant swagger and salty tang. I don't care how 'bogus' the old sea dog yarns are, they still read brilliantly. *The Journal — Paul Sutton*

REICH STUFF [1]

Check it out: two curb crawling toots cash down,
that siren cry creeping up from steam seeping sidewalk,
enraptured preacher rant, "And they crucified Jesus ... And they ...
cru-ci-fied — Jesus/Jesus" blare of horn two car crashes
down from subway shuffle, keyboards now, maybe then, percussive,
some heart beat, beat attack, pulse-blood, synchronized heart,
analogued, made to music by excerpts — Check it out.

Noise, omnipresent Sunday school teaching attributes
to something unknown, some sane search for silence
in the gaps and lapse mayhem orchestrated, lives lived
in waves, registered, re-mastered. Sirens again —
same sirens? (Pause — stutter of silence)
Gun shots. Car backfires. Screech of bald tyres.
Some shout in the street — not God.
Some gentle chord progression — simple
augmented canons. Street vendor ad lib reverb,
hit reverse tape technique. Echo. Echo like a pulse,
toothache in the bed of beat. Making sense in the music,
sensing this making — recording levels maladjusted.

Noise in head, lashed to the mast, some siren cry,
crashing against, waves, cosine wave, sometimes tangential
signal against, on and with, so much data, soundboard skyscrapers,
draw near, wash away, tied to the mast, onrush sirens cry.
Noise in the head, rambling, like Monk — yeah, maybe just like Monk
one time he in the night, in his night, dancing shuffling to the beat
of car lights pulsing back blackness — check it out.

Sirens cry
draw near

---

[1]Originally published on-line by some mag State-Side/New York
based, I think, lost all references to it, about 1998 – perhaps? I
wasn't even on-line at the time, a friend posted it up – saw it
while down the library, surfed for half an hour, took twenty-eight
minutes to find it, was thrown off after half an hour, never saw it
again, but muckle thanks to person or persons unknown.

draw against
and disappear:
rush
onrush
moving in, move it out,
out there city spat

check it out.

PASSING SHIPS [13]

I had a blister on the end of ma toe
for a whole month. I wouldn't pop it.
Shewed everyone it, just for a dare,
just to make 'em think, just for a minute,
how truly inefficient is the human body.

I suppose it got bored, couldn't
cope with the strange adulation
of strangers, eyeing it up as I pulled
off my sock; I suppose, there was a whole
world to see, career opportunities down
south, perhaps it had a sole mate somewhere,
near Fife or Grimsby, somewhere on the East
Coast. I suppose it is none of ma business,
but I noticed one morning towelling masel' off
just after a kebab that it had gone and gone
for good. I spent a whole fortnight stopping folk
in the street and taking off ma sock, they
couldn't find a fault, but by the way they
moved off down the street, I knew they
knew that there was something deeply wrong,
perhaps it is time for a committee or a quango
to sort this human body thing out once and for all.

NO AMBITION *for Moni who has a point*

she weighed both sides of my
brain's lobes with her fingernails,
supposed them lacking
she said my bank balance can't
raise it
she said my expectations were low
she said we were never going to make it
she said my feelings were stunted
she said my pension plans
were past it
she said my sperm count was down
she said my ganja garden
wouldn't grow
she said my portions were small,
that I cheated on the salad, she
said I cheated on her sister, mother
and the window cleaner next door
she said if my love was a mustard
seed it couldn't move dust
she said my academic record was
a scratched 45 and no 12 inch special
said that I was happy living
the life that I was living:
the mould, the rat
and the six month short-hold
she said she had said all this before
she said enough but I wanted more

Counterfeiting Charity Status

When you're homeless as hell
wiping your arse on the Big Issue
held inside by a tissue of lies
cracking the lice with your nails
stuffing your boots with junk-mail
leaflets for energy-saving
or saving the whale
and tramps give you ten pence
for a cup of meths
all your best friends get to be clichés
like get a life
get a wife
get a knife
take your life
and see what you can get for it,
just doff your cap and beg
and if pennies should fall from heaven
don't forget to bite 'em to taste, to test,
their metal —
smile your rusty smile
and sell out quick,
while you still got teeth.

NUMEROLOGY: DOMINOES WITH GRANDMA [14]

I took again the wooden-box from the cupboard,
blew away the film of dust and shuffled dead bones.
Her hands, fingers, gripping the pieces,
knots of time tied in veins.
Big Ben: fortune
one-six: a traveller's domino
one-five: bad luck
six-five: the priest
double five: a curse —
making end to end, fifteen the devil's number.
I'm knocking, rapping the table: —

Grandma rambling, her first mother;
a name, not even a photograph ingrained in sepia,
she remembers the day they came for her

five-two: a partner
double-two: the lovers

and an Aunt from Canada had called
found my Grandma's mother sticking pins in her head.

two-six: an important letter
I'm knocking; rap the table.

She had a brain tumour,
but no one knew
so they took her screaming,
frothing her children's names from bit lips.

five-three: wealth
three-one: for a son
double one: twins
one-blank: spinster

Home from the pit,
her father went unwashed to the infirmary

I'm knocking, rapping the table,
Grandma talking.

84

They wouldn't let him
to see her.

Five-four: policeman
Double-four: midwife

A cleaner found her dead,
died blind and in pain

double-blank: for eternity.

OI YE OF LITTLE DECONSTRUCTION

for all the whinging postmodernists
making a healthy living off the death of God
dearly holding their, where was Jahova
at Auschwitz party card

let me tell you, sonny,
God was there, right on time
stoking the fires, laying on the gas
laying out the corpses

Man, you should ken
God just had to be there
he's good like that

Mistaking Myself for the Irreverent Ian Paisley [15]

It wasn't that easy kicking the Pope downstairs,
wearing only Achilles' heels and nineteen forties
type bathing trunks. And if I was justified by faith
alone, I hadn't a prayer, interrupting the Pope,
ex cathedra, pontificating in the bathroom, taking
the piss out of ma rubber-duck and the state of ma
soul, bedding down in the linen basket wi' ma
dirty duds, stinking socks and spoiled vestments.
I never meant to kick the Pope downstairs wearing
only Achilles' heels, tottering to the brink of Kierkegaard's
leap of faith, watching that dithering Pole bang and bash his
way downstairs, still clutching a report in three persons
on Vatican two: Scunthorpe United 0:
and a dirty pair of boxer shorts with naked
nuns on the back, a present from Lourdes
from my x-mother-in-law, who'd gone there to cure
her alopecia and for fresh country air. Still, enough,
there was Il Papa, Christ's representative on earth,
fumbling with the catch of ma front door, searching
for a way out, the poor sod forgetting that all roads
lead to Rome, even the road to Damascus or a road
paved with good intentions, as I pick up ma Jesus
sandals, a *Betterware* catalogue from the doormat,
as I limp after God's favourite pensioner, making sure
that he gets on the bus round the corner, asking for
forgiveness, begging for a mustard seed, down on ma hands
and Achilles' heels for the return of ma second-best
boxer shorts...

Amen, go in peace,
and have the right change handy, it helps.

A GRANDAD EXPLAINS SODOMY IN YORKSHIRE

Ee, lad, we couldn't afford KY jelly in Batley,
we saved us best dripping from't Sunday Roast
and thought none the worse for it, and if tha were
thrifty, there woh even some left for't rest of the week,
'aving it cold on Monday, possibly Tuesday, a sarnie
or two for bait box, for't snap, for't Wednesday,
by time Thursday came along it woh Shepherd's Pie,
An' Friday, of course, woh freshly battered fish supper,
a big fry Saturday morning, and afore you know it, lad,
it woh Sunday again an' buggering abart wi' dripping
pot, a spit of god in a wine cup and bit o' bread
to mop it all up, sodomy, damnation in a flat cap,
copious parsimony, back o' father's hand,
and by hell we were glad on it, allus saw life sunny side up
in them days when we add nowt but mekking us own
entertainment sat round watching an ald
valve wireless warm up,
and we never heard the word obesity
not in them days
never been
so well

stuffed.

POETRY OF LITTLE THINGS

Julie said she thought that she had
just given birth to a wet fart but
not to worry. I worried.
On this week's special offer sheet
there was half a leg of lamb
going cheap and a barbecue
set for the once in a lifetime
price of £14.98 inclusive of vat,
but there was no proviso for
unwanted anal discharge:
worrying or not.

She spent the day ganning round the
Metro Centre with her Mam and her
outsize see-through plastic bag. I filled
in a free competition to win a family saloon
in Texas; I whupped that bit of paper across the room,
I tore it into bits, made it beg for the waste —
basket and I didn't even have a family
or a clean driving licence.

Julie was drinking her Mam under the table.
It was comfy down there despite dubious stains,
cig-burns and the glare she got off her handbag,
it sawed right through her and didn't like what it saw.
I thought how time passes between seconds,
laggardly, limping and so coldly, despite insolation
and the lack of cloud cover, but that's Northumberland
for you and the 518 bus was late too, mindst.

It was a good bit after tea because the dogs had
finished licking the plates when Julie arrived
back, with various packages and the statement
about what she had done to her knickers. I, still
worrying, asked how her Mam was bee
keeping. She had her bag stolen. That's life I said
and we both agreed on that, of that I am most
sure about as the seconds ticked by without
a ray of hope as Julie searched the cupboard bare
below the kitchen sink for out of date
stain remover, as she too

began to worry.

COO-PUNCHING

Try to talk it through
stumbling through
the wood of words
drunk as a caterpillar not seeing
the forest for the leaves
worried that John Wayne
killed too many Indians
leaving nothing to scalp
but the faded print of porno
magazine-snagged
on a barbed-wired keep out
sign, worried that God
might still be about with
some of that guilt and
the shout of ma father
promising to sort me
out, just like a sheriff,
just like that fat bastard
John Wayne drinking
blood and whiskey
with the cut out cunt
of squaw over the stock
of his barrel of laughs
in the quiet man, that
fight up the street
that made ma Gran
laugh her false teeth into
her handkerchief, as
Grandad tried to remember
where his hands were on
his neighbour's piano, wondering whether
he was a kafflick or kommunist
or just a bad pianist, playing
the international like a double reel,
as Desperate Dan looks like the man
from the Pru, talking it into the letter-box

that no one is in, especially if the
bailiffs are asking, that ma mam
has run off with the milkman,
a blackman, mayhaps even an Indian,
leaving her stiletto in ma father's scalp
still threatening to come back
to sort it out, hunting his trail
through the badly packed suitcase,
the bus stop on the corner, shouting
Jeronimo at that purple belch of
diesel, running off into the dull
street yonder, not stopping
till fields, then woods, put up
a last stand against street, house
corner, end terrace, finding
a tail feather of a pheasant,
tucking it up into ma preoccupations,
worried that John Wayne just might be
God or his best marra,
wandering over the pass home,
lonely as a cowboy song no
one can sing, especially me
who is through
with words, even the right ones,
spitting ma hate like a snake
with ma tongue in bits,
forked off with it all, finding something
sinisterly noble in that redundant
gesture of no surrender
printed on the posse pack
of ma Orange playing cards.

4 What the Butler Sawed

Took the train to Huddersfield for two and half
years to receive a M.A. in poetry, during
which I did not write a single verse — Man,
that course sure taught me.

Thank you for sending us your lively and unusual poems.
Seren — Amy Wack

BACK TOGETHER [16]

a back-to-back council house,
minding the weeds, taking care
of grafitti, cat-shit and stray
junk mail with pram wheels —
so much unloved bricks and mortar
held together

someone put him to live there
came once a week to make sure...
he was still struggling with
soap, flannel, a comb through the hair
his only other visitor
came to read the electric meter

some scum armed with a spray-can
blasted *nonce* on his garden wall
finished him in car-paint blue,
shuffling to the shops the calls begin
shit through the letter-box, smashed
windows, set fire to his dustbin
holding him down to kick him in

they fucked that idiot over
the fuckwit from the looney bin
half a mind and that a bairn
found him spitting blood and nursery
rhymes by the nonce narked wall
and all I kent and ken
couldn't put
numpty dumpty
back together again

BURNING, BURNING [17]

guilty as the centre
what elsing wailing
these words, never
wake no dead, prepare
the wirecutters, sharpen
every night, sing these
blues, kill that thought,
ride that beat, this scalpel
sound, oh ... you know it,
by then, it over, by then
cut short, all the bits
left, crude cuts,
to mouth over, like braille,
spitting out, typical,
what elsing wailing,
blister of words,
stuck guilty
centre

HER LIFE AS A MAN [18]

I'm not saying it was easy,
shouldn't say anything,
just the way she slunk out of bed,
her bottom not full, not pear,
not apple, not part of some
collection from a fruit bowl,
narrow and honed as desire.

She pulled on stockings, heard
the small pricks of hard hair,
fighting against the grain,
working their way out from
her, betraying, stiff as frost-
killed birds. She ran

her fingers across my chest,
kissed the hand, stroked the hand,
pulled her back to me, cupped
the hard, tight nipple of her heart
and kissed. Next door's gate clicked,
she said something about it was time

she was gone. She touched me then,
made me come again, some morning's
drowsy orgasm, stale heat sickly sweet.
More tired than tired, aching to find
something with which to say goodbye,
watched her leave, attired safely,

inconspicuous as a stereotype. I
wouldn't say it was easy for her,
wouldn't even begin to say that.

FIXING A SONNET TO SING A LULLABY [19]

You place the small cracked mirror, smeared
with rust blots and seven years bad luck,
you find the image of someone that might
have been, could have been, you, wearing
that being there, done it, *Dasein* designer t-shirt,
though rolling up the sleeves of your long
black, ageless black poller-neck to tie
your old school tie around your elbow,
nudging good health and sage practise
out of the way, to good effect, nothing popping
up in vein, see the smirk of your own pun,
have fun, teaspoon hot and ready with
Grandma's best buttercup syrup —
"Two sugars, Sir Henry, and a piece of tiffin?"
hot flush, double flush, clean-clean as a toilet
detergent advert right round the bend
the glow on your face nay deterrent,
nor the later pallor and dull dead eyes,
see what the pathologist will see, know what that
expert will know and ken too that self-knowledge
is never what it's cracked up to be, one dead
smart-arse is still a morgue-slab bum,
and, anyway, what you want? Poetry?
If that's what you want, how much
a line you willing to pay?

Time on your Beer [20]

Took off ma glasses the other day and ma head fell off,
smashed on't pavement like, nay fit state to be ganning
anywhere, though made it into *The Schooner* for the karioke
just the same, which is unusual as I don't sing, but had a pint
nonetheless, asked for a big head just like back in Yorkshire,
they didn't pour it right and couldn't pay and someone
in the corner singing all the rude, alternative rude,
words to a Jimmy Rogers song, asked me did I know him
from somewhere. Actually, knew the gaje from nowhere,
till he said, so these 'ere aren't your glasses then, throwing
a dark pair of seventies shades to the floor. Groped, I went
down on ma hands and knees and god wasn't even behind
the bar and found what was left of ma face and walked out the
wrong door, just like John Wayne, only smaller as the barman
called time a relative concept, time called him a relatively
fat bloater, knew, right down to the second hand, that soon
I was overdue as a lost library book down the doctors for
something more than an out of date sick-note, struggling
back inside pint-pot glasses, ma anonymous self with the
years left hugging the face like a broken toilet seat,
wanting to gan hame, just forget, forget about some of it
d.n.a, mr multi-verse and the ill-nature of time, swallowed
whole by a black hole, leaving yours truly with only
seconds to spare and nay pension plan of ma own, for when
they retire me, at long last, after forty years hard
service on the bru, doing the double, down the dole.

Right Change

All modern tears
ardent in their warnings
distill everly in false
melancholy, elgiac as erased
figures, totalling idly in
the margins, sums forfeited
from sight, a landscape
falsely figured in loaned
Arabaic abeyance to this
rough tongue, licking the
edge of phonemes, inventive
as a coughed splutter, spat
on the frosted air —
cosmopolitan as a bus-stop.

9 SECOND AVENUE, AMBLE

it's hard shitting with
an eviction notice hung
around your neck
swinging this way or
that, throwing you off balance

gone are the days when
I could leave a
place with just a rut-sack and carrier bag
finding at need some gap in the hedge to
let loose my stools then to make the
best use of stray leaves or thrown porn mags
in those days on the road
you shat with makeshift ease

these days, I've got this big
wardrobe, antique, large enough for
ma manservant, dresser, gentleman's
gentleman, it's big, put it on wheels and
live in it — man, it's big enough to
take a shit in it

like ah said, it's hard to let go
an eviction notice hung on the clodgy door
hard, but not impossible

Where's the Tatties?

I've been doing it for years
all this hands and knees stuff
worn out three pairs of trousers
have rheumatism enough
in both patellas.

I've turned the other cheek
had it slapped, kicked
and tattooed on the cheap
both sides, Fred O'Stare style
dancing cheek to cheek.

I've never coverted my neighbour's
ass or goat or three piece suite,
never mind the offers
special offers too, mindst ye,
coupons and condoms.

There's more, aye, aye
dentures to dentures stuff
but I've had enough, see,
even if the lad Jesus,
is the lamb of God...

I'm the *mint sauce.*

TOWARDS THE LIGHT

There were shadows in the field
fleet, nimble, thick with the scent of night
sudden eye of a cigarette tightly held
lost in the dark some sudden squeal of fright,

we moved lumbering as moles, twice as blind,
to find the ald lurcher bitch caught in wire
the beat of her heart warming the frozen ground
in the burst of torchlight her blood warm as fire;

we worked quickly, cursing and cutting, knowing
she was lost, even as her pup came to us
the hunched rabbit dead in its jaws, spittle foaming
with the slavver of self-praise, watching us

cut its mother's throat, her body free
as the day fell to snowing, covering our tracks,
as carried between us we turned to home in the dree
dawn grey warmed by the sole chorus of a dog-fox.

21st CENT OEDIPUS WRECKED [21]

You have it all wrong
they blinded me, burnt
ma eyes for looking at
ma mother's cunt
and liking it. They
couldn't stand to see
that. Ah stood, stood
and killed the man
who was ma father,
knifed him in the alley
cos what he did to ma
designer shoes. As he lay
spilling his blood
I said, look who's fuck-
ing Mama now — he neva
smiled. You have it
wrong, plagues and shit,
the gods just hated
ma luck, they fucked
each other sense-
less for aeons
wanting worshipping for it,
neva ending up as some
quick quip for black rap
gangster milking the whigger
market, the gods hated
the way that ah was king.

And, lastly, you got it wrong
about the suicide of ma wife.
Ah killed her, wanting some
fresh cut of gash than her
ald slit, maybe fuck her
daughter, keeping it all
family, like the royalty
of Europe or ancient Egypt.

They took ma eyes. They
took a name for ma feet
and walked ma crippled name right
down into the deepest fears
of their blind psychology — scared
ah was fucking their mothers too.

5 Colour of Fluff

when you can't sing
you write
when you can't write
you mime
... if you can't mime
apply for an arts' grant.

AN X- AMPLE [22]

an x rang me up
while I was away in Hull
doing a reading to ask
if she could come round
and commit suicide

getting back I rang her back
told her dad that I wasn't
interested, he cried,
said he'd allus thought of me
as the son he never had,
though a bit smaller

she rang again on Tuesday
said was there anybody else
available, there wasn't
she made me promise
to call her back — x-directory
when I changed ma mind

I changed the sheets on Saturday,
took a change of heart on Sunday
on Monday the police came
to identify the body
it was still ma body
labelled exhibit E
they left, without wiping their feet

as for the x
she has a job now in what was *Safeways*
safe-hands; still nursing regrets
still alive

if you like this poem,
send a small donation to the
Samaritans, and if you don't
ring them

HOT-DOGGING [23]

you finger your clitoris
I am excited
I wish you wouldn't
do this at the dentist's

I tell you I have responsibilities now
that I have joined three book clubs
and must buy a book from each brochure
for the next three score and ten

you are not bothered
it hurts

I still enjoy sucking your cunt
but why insist on this
queueing late at night
for a six-seater taxi

you pull me off the seat by ma hair
which is unusual as I shave ma head
you wipe ma lips over your tits
while people get on and off the clapped-out
bus

I am hurting still
you are not bothered

you ask me to make love in the shower
I warn that it could fair up at any minute
and the Sunday Market is quite busy
it does not stop you fingering ma arse

my doctor told me that I had six minutes to live
I waited ten just for a prescription
you told me you had found another man
in the animal sanctuary charity shop in Alnwick

I am hurt
you are not bothered

this is

AT THE END OF SLIME

They said Slug had no spine, dusted off in a new jacket, munching sub-text, inter-text and the texture of paper word-thin. They said Slug didn't belong, feeding on the classics; worms shunned him, well-read, fed and bloated with learning. Slug, they sandwiched him between the East Europeans and Critical Theory, catching him working out in his new Jean Francoise Lyotard. Slug, poor Slug-Worm, it wasn't what they said that signified, just the way they held his head steadfast by his tentacles, as they slit his throat, spilling blood, clotted with ikons. Just like Kafka, they said at last — and again.

ON THE PISS WITH JIM KEOGH

They threw away his application to join The Welsh Academy,
the Magic Circle and the Todmordern Taliban. He got a booking.
He was late, by several decades still stuck on punk,
despite total hairloss, and despite his linguistic baggage
of tricks, he was still no Debbie Magee. He was though drunk.

He got up on stage by his hands and knees, scattering one-liners
like confetti, handing out gags and condoms and some offers
on Pizza Hovel, it was his regular work, when poems were not
in season, he warmed up with a low IQ Haiku, couldn't count

his syllables or where fell the end of the line. Still,
he was still holding it together, bit of tarpaulin rope
tied around his middle, as he dropped the crown on a sonnet
series about Scunthorpe, juggling with the microphone, no

laughs, not even from the can of cask-conditioned Dandelion
and Burdock. Started to sweat, started to shake an infirm
terza rima to a rhyme and Blues number, 36, panicked, changed
tack, doing impressions, but never a performance poet.

Dropped his kegs, let loose his trews, no underpants
turning round, touching toes, exposing the rim of his arse
pulling back his cheeks, cracking off some street-wise poetry
Do you know who it is yet? Rhetorical, Roger McBoff!

Back with one-liners, back at his stool at the bar.
No bard, this man. Nothing even close. A woman took pity
brought his trews off the stage, made him put them on. It wasn't Debbie
Magee. It wasn't anything you'd call poetry.

TOO TIRED TO SHIT

There was a party going, but I wasn't drinking
anything but alcohol, there was drugs in buckets
but I was doing nothing but alcohol, till my mate Bill
mixed speed and real ale, called it ma special brew
every time I would drop ma head he'd walk on through
bring me another bucket, there was a woman who they said
was interested in me, I found her in bed with Bill
who afterwards brought me another special brew.
"Sorry, kiddah." No problemo, I'd smashed all his records
put them back in their sleeves and pissed in his breakfast
cereal. Besides, I still liked that special brew. Someone
started a fight. It was me. I got tired and bored, afore
it was half-way through, kept wrapping ma arms Fred's head
closed me eyes wanting a kip more than a scrap, till Bill
came through with another special brew. Man it was tops
as I slapped Fred in the chops, kicked him in the knacs
then threw his jacket out the window, while his was wearing
it still. Bill confessed he'd added Angel Dust in with the rest.
Man, I was pissed, but still up for it, as we boogied outside
taking turns to do a seventies' shimmy-shammy down the kids' slide
till I tired, crashing on the lilo but barely for a wink or two
as Bill propped up ma elbow with another special brew.
I was whizzing, I was fizzing, the girl that wanted me, found
that I would do, giving me a good seeing to, even though
whether fast or slow I couldn't cum despite her sucks, despite
some blow that Bill blew through ma special brew. I shagged
for hours through, the end of ma cock looked ready to drop-off
perhaps super-glue would do, as Bill used it to stir ma special
brew, adding some crushed tabs of viagra and home-made voodoo.
Did the trick as ma dick spewed, no woman in sight, but some head
on ma special brew. Man I was flagging and the ale was all gone
and I don't drink lager except on the continent where they ken
how to brew. Someone called the filth, they turned us over, a
stupid thing to do, as they took the phone off me along with ma
belt and shoelaces and and ma Mr Magoo glasses and still couldn't

111

sleep as I lay in ma cell with Bill, snoring from both ends
in the bunk above me, pausing only to puke in the sink and take a
drink from the loo. They let me go at around a quarter to nine
when there was a change of crew giving me back ma laces and belt
but no trews, as I marched on home, feeling ill to sit on ma loo
too tired to shit. I was going to say poo, but man I hate an
easy end rhyme
          scheme.

NANCARROW'S WHEELBARROW

No phonemes thrived in my garden,
no sound of plosives, no bird song
not even my rare collection of Czech C
over by trained trailing structure
of my syntax, that and all the vowels
punched out and rolling; this Babel
this out-timed stutter of what we do
with words, arranged and re-arranged
with sentences left unclaimed, and just
like Candide, I take my thumb and begin
to shovel, the best of all possible
arrangments into my Nancarrow wheelbarrow
crank up the organ and watch the monkeys
dance across of the as-yet unformed thoughts,
snatches of sentences, spiralling off into
the middle distance of tomorrow.

PARTY ANIMAL

There's a party in my head
everyone high and drunk
out of order
everyone is me.

I call last orders
that's when the riot starts
but no police ever come,
in the free for all that follows
it's last madman standing.

And I limp off to bed at last,
blooded as a caught fox, lost,
more than I've won, but
in my maddest moments,
it's fun.

COMPULSIVE LIGHT

If I slapped every lamppost in the street
everything would be all right.
Lining them up rigid as a firing squad,
one a fraction out. It troubles me
to slap it twice.

Street curves and a straggler
lurches into view. I slap.
The bend bulges to a junction,
line divided with light,
mad as a pup chasing flies,
I slap all light, follow a new chain,
projected in the dim curve of distance.

I run the stream of lights,
hard slapping back the dark,
to find my fingers broken
my luck doused yet ill-shod
beneath the orange halo,
flickering neon,
that can't stay touched.

Still

Storm passes,
I shore up what is left of the head,
prop up some doll, figure of person,
to send back out there, to discover,
to identify remains, as the cracks
in the wall, spread and splinter
to the sound of breaking bone,
I find a shade of quiet enough to capture
a sense of still ... a fractured
moment where the great shout
of the brain is frozen,
mid-grimace, caught almost
smiling, as winds quicken.

LIVING SOME LIFE [24]

Living mi life like a background artist
of a Shane Meadows' movie and liking it.
Giving everyone ma autograph: the man at the brú,
bailiffs and rack-renters, my probation officer Pru
dence.

I asked the man at the bookies,
Where's the money, Ronny?
he shook his head and said,
just move along, sonny, which was uncanny,
fitting in with the dead-end rhyme-scheme
of ma poem, though nay richer, oss shot at
Doncaster, should have run faster,
despite this disaster, ma outlook is sunny
some scattered showers moving west, entering
this vale of tears by mourning — geography
some other subject I failed
at Borstal's juvenile jail.

Mi life left hang
-ing, de-
railed ... waiting for an equity card
dead scared 'cos I can't do regional accents.

Madness in ma method acting, a fat bastard
Marlon Brando queing at the soup kitchen:
Lights, action, camera! [1]

---

[1] Over 2000 poems now, charva, go on, write another poem taking
the Micheal

117

Where Published

[1] Niall McGrath ed. Changing channels. *Black Mountain Review*, 4:84, 2001.

[2] Peter Knaggs ed. Hand of maradonna. *Slab*, 1, 2004.

[3] Paul Sutherland ed. Home shopping. *Dream Catcher*, 15:71, 2005.

[4] Nigel Bird ed. Chinask's shanty. *The Rue Bella — Busted Flat*, 8:53, 2002.

[5] Paul Sutherland ed. 2 sugars but no milk. *Dream Catcher*, 15:12, 2005.

[6] Peter Knaggs ed. Hull revisited reluctantly. *Slab*, 1, 2004.

[7] Sam Smith ed. Éirígí suas brigantaighe. *The Journal of Contemporary Anglo-Scandinavian Poetry*, 4, 1996.

[8] Shane Rhodes ed. The kipper's shanty. *The Reater*, 4, 2001. appeared on the attached cdrom.

[9] Daithidh MacEochaidh & Gareth Spark. *Ramraid For Beginners*. Skrev Press, 15 Pwllhai, CARDIGAN, 2nd edition, 2003.

[10] Mark Robinson ed. Breaking the ice at a monday club soiree. *Scratch — Invisible Spin Doctors*, 16:23–25, 1997.

[11] Peter Knaggs ed. To obsess. *Slab*, 1, 2004.

[12] Paul Sutherland ed. Junk mail. *Dream Catcher*, 15:23, 2005.

[13] Nigel Bird ed. Passing ships. *Rue Bella*, 9:43, 2002.

[14] Kerry Sowerby ed. Numerology with grandma. *Ramraid Extraordinaire*, page 81, 1995.

[15] Niall McGrath ed. Mistaking myself for the irreverant ian paisley. *Black Mountain Review*, 6:46, 2002.

[16] Beth Rudkin ed. Back together. *Acorn*, 6:54, 2003.

[17] Paul Sutherland ed. Burning, burning. *Dream Catcher*, 11:66, 2003.

[18] Paul Sutherland ed. Her life as a man. *Dream Catcher*, 11:67, 2003.

[19] Nigel Bird ed. Fixing a sonnet to sing a lullabye. *Rue Bella*, 7:106, 2001.

[20] Nigel Bird ed. Time on your beer. *Rue Bella*, 7:107, 2001.

[21] Peter Knaggs ed. 21st cent oedipus wrecked. *Slab*, 1, 2004.

[22] Peter Knaggs ed. An x- ample. *Slab*, 1, 2004.

[23] Peter Knaggs ed. Hot-dogging. *Slab*, 1, 2004.

[24] Cathy Grindrod. Living some life. *Poetry Nottingham International*, 55(1):21, 2002.

Information & Other Titles

Like a Dog to its Vomit — Daithidh MacEochaidh

If you only buy one experimental novel in your life-time,
buy this one – the author needs the brass.

Daithidh MacEochaidh

Somewhere between the text, the intertext and the testosterone find Ron Smith,
illiterate book lover, philosopher of non-thought and the head honcho's left-arm
man. Watch Ron as he oversees the begging franchise on Gunnarsgate, shares
a room with a mouse of the Lacota Sioux and makes love to Tracy, back from the
dead and still eager to get into his dungarees. There's a virgin giving birth under
the stairs, putsch at the taxi rank and Kali, Goddess of Death, is calling. Only
Arturo can sort it, but Arturo is travelling. In part two, find out how to live in a sock,
and select sweets from a shop that time forgot, and meet a no-holds barred state-
registered girlfriend. In part three, an author promises truth, but the author is dead
— isn't she?

In this complex, stylish and downright dirty novel, MacEochaidh belts through un-
derclass underachieving, whilst committing postmodern, post-it notes to the page,
pausing only to savour the more pungent bodily orifices en route to a total textual
breakdown that is the end ... perhaps.

route ISBN 1-901927-07-5 £6.95

Half a Pint of Tristram Shandy

'... three young poets whose verse is diverse, provocative, brave and original. Between the leaves of this book lies the mad, boundless energy of the globe cracking up under our very noses; it is a world which is harnessed in images of jazz, sex, drugs, aliens, abuse, in effective colloquial language and manic syntax, but the themes are always treated with gravity, unsettling candour, and humour.'

Jack Mapanje

Poetry should be constantly refreshing itself, constantly updating itself with new voices and perspectives, and that's just what this book does. Here are three poets with new angles on old themes, new angles on very personal themes, and, dammit, lines that I wish I'd thought of.

Ian MacMillan

Four Star Review — The Big Issue

I'm happier with MacEochaidh's *Don't Let Death Move In*. The difference is the poet's pyrotechnic wit, which finds rich irony and great laughs in the same situations. His deftness of touch means that when he lets his anger off the leash, the effect is brilliantly explosive.

If you're looking for avant garde, look no further — the contemporary scene of drugs, sex and rock n' roll, aliens, abuse, all the concerns of generation X ... Daithidh MacEochaidh is whimsical in a bitter way, his erudition shines through. One to watch surely.

Casey Flynn, *The Black Mountain Review*

The serrated edge of the vernacular tongue can be found in Blake Morrison's Oedipus, ... in Simon Nye's Don Juan ... It can also be savoured in Daithidh MacEochaidh's own poems in *Half a Pint of Tristram Shandy* —

Artscene

£6.95 ISBN 1-901927-156

121

Solipsism For Beginners — Dai Parsons & Daithidh MacEochaidh

This is an experiment in dirty fiction. A book unlike ANY in the Guardian Review — Artscene

The ability of these two writers to consistently create interesting philosophical stories is amazing. They take you with them into the streets and into the lives their characters inhabit, embrace the reader in the worlds they have created so convincingly you just lose yourself there, and feel it is your own world, one you have always known.

Sonja McGarr, *The Black Mountain Review*

ISBN 1-904646-01-8 £9.99 €16.99 $16.99

Ramraid — Daithidh MacEochaidh & Gareth Spark

Two Full Collections for the Price of One

Spark's writing is tender, angry and wonderfully observational, as in the "The Four Month Midnight" about Scoresby, the famous Whitby explorer...

Daithidh MacEochaidh's poems are delightfully wordy, swimming in the deep end of the language baths. I'm rereading Kerouac for the "Big Read", and it seems that MacEochaidh shares some of his linguistic exuberance. More power to him!

Ian McMillan

Spark has a style and a poetic instinct that are second to none. He is a poet who deserves to be lauded as one of the best in Britain today. Spark for my money is as good as Armitage or Duffy any day.

MacEochaidh: his tongue-in-cheek, streetwise style is familiar, yet it masks a brooding intellect of enormous weight and exactitude. The energy and scope of his consciousness   amaze
...the poet combines, and at the same time explores, deep philosophical questions in beautiful imagery.

The Black Mountain Review

There's nothing in Daithidh MacEochaidh's aspirant fiction that had prepared us for *Ramraid*. The book harbours a miscellany of previously published poetry whose calibre is unmistakable; MacEochaidh evokes memories and focuses on hypnoid states with a clarity and economy that is born of wide reading, personal struggle and tough self-editing.

Artscene

ISBN 978-1-904646-34-1 £6.99 €18.99 $18.99

Islands in Time — Daithidh MacEochaidh

A dark atmospheric novel that trades on Gothic tropes, as it draws upon place, narrative and myth. Nordic and Celtic elements fuse to create a world that hinges the humdrum of now and a lost past. The *Whicker Man* meets *Local Hero* in a modern arc of damnation and fate.

... The Characters, their relationships and plot will compel you to read this strangely heart-warming "arc of damnation and fate." — *The Black Mountian Review*

ISBN1-904646-16-6 £9.99 €18.99 $18.99

Travels with Chinaski | Daithidh MacEochaidh

In literature, the flaunting of influences can be a treacherous business. Come up short in the shadow of your muse and you risk being seen as some kind of eternal bare-faced second-rater. Thankfully, that's not the case though with Daithidh MacEochaidh who knows how to manipulate and play with Bukowski's anti-hero, to create a raw and truthful collection of poems for Wrecking Ball Press, taking us willingly on a journey through love and squalor and "the small windows with which those bedsits were framed", to booze-hell and back. "Black mould on the walls, no heating, nothing in but drink, we had those hours cold as turkey, shivering into our alcohol."

Dogmatika

Wrecking Ball Press ISBN 1-903110-23-8

125

Ramraid | Daithidh MacEochaidh & Gareth Spark

Daithidh MacEochaidh's poems are delightfully wordy, swimming in the deep end of the language baths. I'm rereading Kerouac for the "Big Read", and it seems that MacEochaidh shares some of his linguistic exuberance. More power to him!

Ian McMillan

Spark has a style and a poetic instinct that are second to none. He is a poet who deserves to be lauded as one of the best in Britain today. Spark for my money is as good as Armitage or Duffy any day.

MacEochaidh: his tongue-in-cheek, streetwise style is familiar, yet it masks a brooding intellect of enormous weight and exactitude. The energy and scope of his consciousness amaze ... the poet combines, and at the same time explores, deep philosophical questions in beautiful imagery.

The Black Mountain Review

There's nothing in Daithidh MacEochaidh's aspirant fiction that had prepared us for *Ramraid*. The book harbours a miscellany of previously published poetry whose calibre is unmistakable; MacEochaidh evokes memories and focuses on hypnoid states with a clarity and economy that is born of wide reading, personal struggle and tough self-editing.

Artscene

ISBN1-904646-04-2

126

Liquorish Durg | Daithidh MacEochaidh

A rights of passage, last rights, coming of age in an age of unreason!
It's dead hard growing up UP NORTH, when the pit's shut, when the great dead weight of northern naturalism and social-realism hangs from one's neck like a dead hover hawk, where the only place you know is the past, where the only future is death — a job-experience scheme down at the Cremortorium, when the criminal underworld takes a personal interest in your progress, when your boss is mad, sat up to his neck in a pet's grave, when the only woman you love … loves herself. It's dead tough all right, but Shaun Hardcastle has a crack.

"MacEochaidh deserves to be horsewhipped!"

Major Hopwood-Brown, *The Harrogate Tattler*

SKREV PRESS

edgecities | sean burn | @the edge | sean burn

Two blistering collections of shorter fiction: -

a hilarious elegy to this country, a fucking brilliant barking piece of sanity, epiphany-rant war-zone in-the-streets underground city-sex love song, bigger than bukowski, angrier than kerouac, funnier than anybody, and the lists are genius. always alive, bitter, joyous, warped fizzing justice language, vicious peaceful scared scary anti-blair tender terrrorism for our times, one voice only can do this, that is sean burn, i defy you to read this without crying, laughing, questioning and eating more cake

Matt Black, Author — Plot 161. *Spout*

isbn 978-1-904646-38-9 I isbn 978-1-904646-38-6

sean burn | wings are giving out

a blistering collection of avant garde poetry that makes other poets seem intent on merely producing birthday card verse –

isbn 978-1-904646-56-3

Hanging Johnny

new from Skrev Press: an annual poetry collection seeking everything that is verse today — send up to ten unpublished poems — pays a pound a poem UK only or two copies of the journal — see www.skrevpress.com

SKREV PRESS

Submissions Wanted:

Opportunities for new writers — Skrev seeks new writing: -

poetry
short stories
collections of poetry
collections of stories
novellas
novels
plays
special commissions

Contact Skrev

David Morley on Skrev Press
Director of Warwick Writing Programme
University of Warwick

Skrev Press, in its various incarnations and imprints, displays an energy and invention in editing which has been lacking in the specialist literary press world since the glory of John Murray's Panurge. The main players in the small press world are doing great things, of course, to the extent they are no longer the small fry but decidedly and healthily mainstream. Well done to them - they serve their readers (and market) well.

Yet isn't something missing — again? Where is the market for short stories, or flash fiction? Where are the young (but unbeautiful) writers who write the difficult (but linguistically glorious) stuff that our current market can't get behind? Have they gone to Mars or turned to advertising?

Skrev Press knows where these writers are; it locates them, edits them and publishes them. In a poverty-stricken kind of way, it even promotes them (which shows certain nobility). On top of that, new writers across the globe are being drawn into Skrev's net by Daithidh MacEochaidh's rigour.

The tradition continues in which a group of fresh writers and a focused editor, united by the desire and single-mindedness to create and promote wonderful new fiction, decide to get annoyed with what's on offer and do it themselves. Maybe in twenty years time, somebody will need to dig it all up again but, for the present, watch Skrev take on the thankless duty of turning the literary ground over.

David Morley Director: Warwick Writing Programme

131

Skrev Press41 Manor Drive
HEBDEN BRIDGE
HX7 8DW
www.skrevpress.com